415 ORIGINAL DESIGNS FOR STAINED GLASS

by Michael Gowen

in association with
Michael Booth
and
Kaleidoscope Art
Glass Studio

DOVER PUBLICATIONS, INC., NEW YORK

Copyright © 1989 by Dover Publications, Inc.
All rights reserved under Pan American and International Copyright Conventions.

Published in Canada by General Publishing Company, Ltd., 30 Lesmill Road, Don Mills, Toronto, Ontario.
Published in the United Kingdom by Constable and Company, Ltd., 10 Orange Street, London WC2H 7EG.

415 Original Designs for Stained Glass is a new work, first published by Dover Publications, Inc., in 1989.

DOVER *Pictorial Archive* SERIES

Manufactured in the United States of America
Dover Publications, Inc., 31 East 2nd Street, Mineola, N.Y. 11501

Library of Congress Cataloging-in-Publication Data

Gowen, Michael.
    415 original designs for stained glass / by Michael Gowen, in association with Michael Booth and Kaleidoscope Art Glass Studio.
        p.   cm. — (Dover pictorial archive series)
    ISBN 0-486-26175-1
    1. Gowen, Michael—Themes, motives. 2. Glass painting and staining—United States—History—20th century—Themes, motives. I. Title. II. Title: Four hundred fifteen original designs for stained glass. III. Series.
NK5398.G68A4   1989
748.5′022′2—dc20   89-38880
                                                                    CIP

Introduction

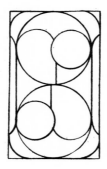

IDAHO-BASED ARTIST MICHAEL GOWEN ardently created original geometric designs for mental exercise, motivated by his love of Art Deco and other modern art genres, before he realized the potential of his work for reproduction in glass. "I then decided to apply a basic rule to my designs," he recalls: "no impossible cuts." The assurance with which he thereafter applied that rule to his work, and generated the windfall of beautiful and functional stained glass designs in the present collection, shows that his highly developed original artistry was awaiting this purpose. Each design herein is a masterful composition of geometric shapes and graceful lines, some of which create special optical effects—yet a glasscutter should find no shape impractical to cut.

The artist himself selected and arranged this exquisite collection of 415 unique designs at Kaleidoscope Art Glass Studio in Boise, Idaho, with the assistance of Michael Booth, an artist associated with the studio. The designs have various outer shapes (some standard geometric, some unique), suitable for the building of windows, transoms, mirrors, boxes, lampcovers and every other type of stained glass project. Even the smallest are readily usable in miniature projects; and with a photostat machine, they can easily be enlarged. Enhanced by the colored glass, setting and amount of light that you choose, these abstract designs can gently complement the contours and hues of surroundings into which they are set, or even resemble gems or natural scenes.

This book is intended as a supplement to stained glass instruction books (such as *Stained Glass Craft* by J. A. F. Divine and G. Blachford, Dover Publications, Inc., 0-486-22812-6). All materials needed for projects, including general instructions and tools for beginners, can usually be purchased from local craft and hobby stores listed in your Yellow Pages.

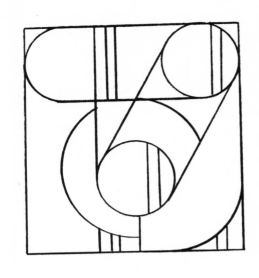

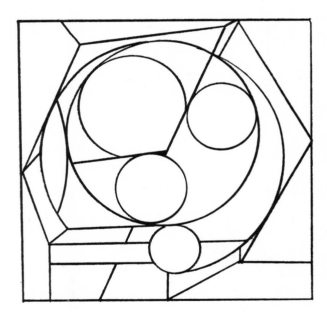

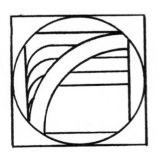

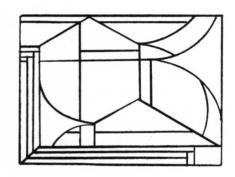

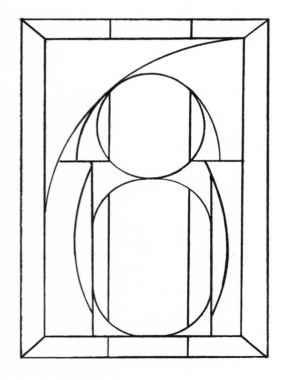

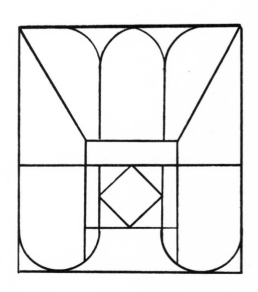

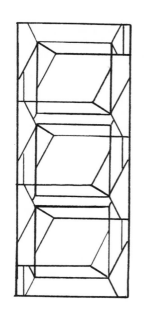
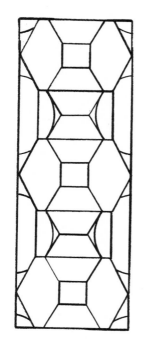

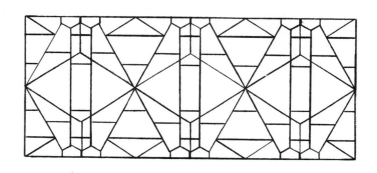

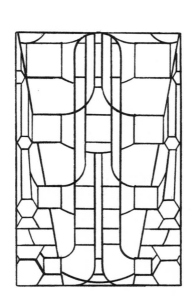

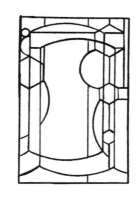
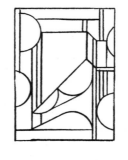
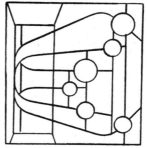
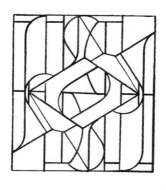

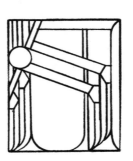
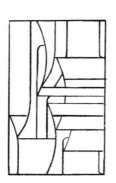

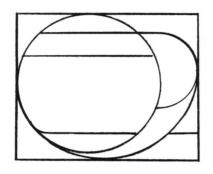

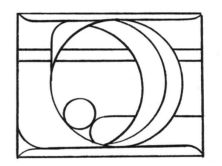

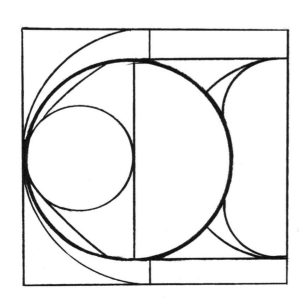

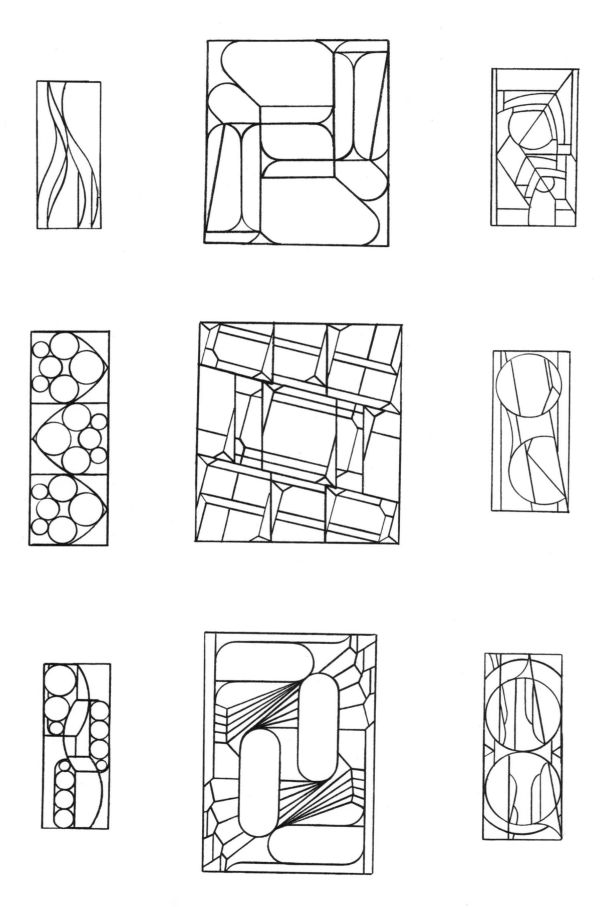

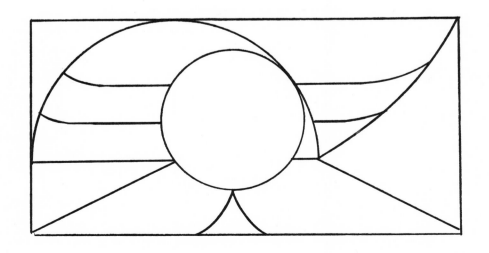

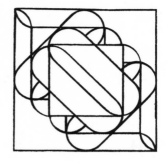

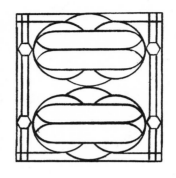

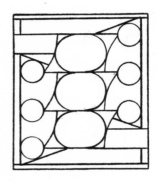

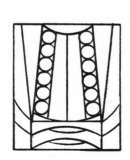

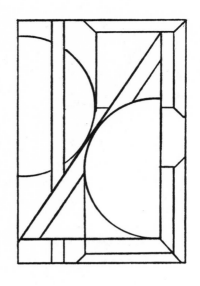

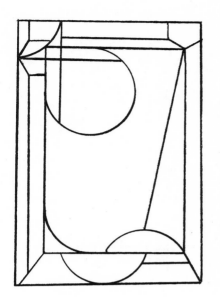

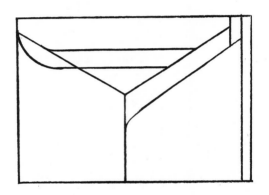

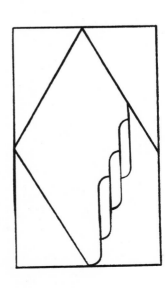

9

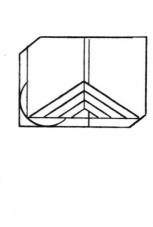
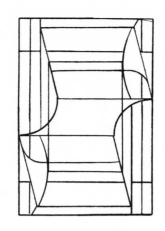
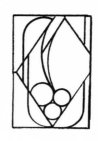
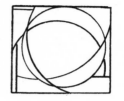
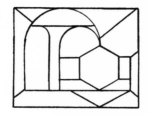

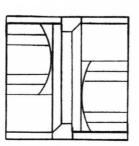

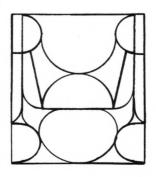
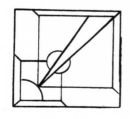

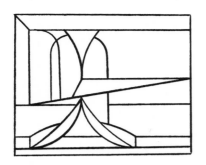

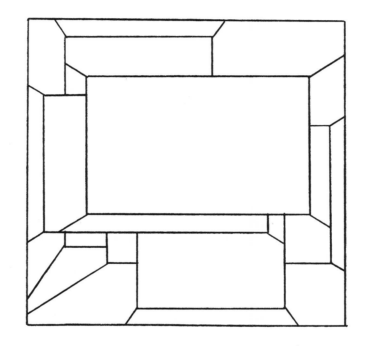

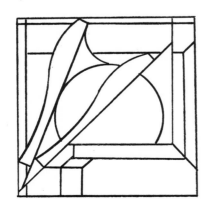

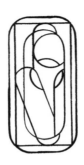

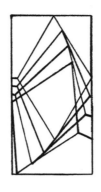

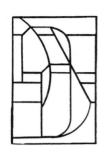

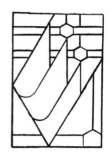

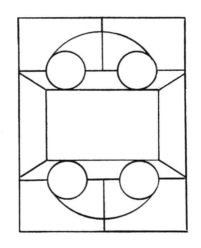

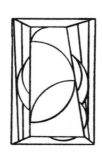

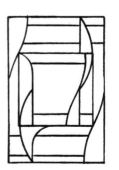

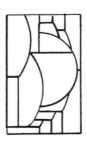

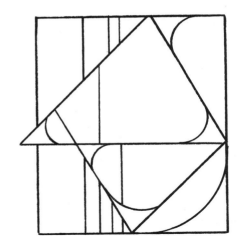

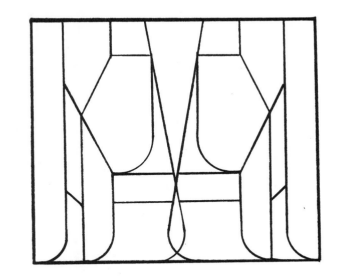

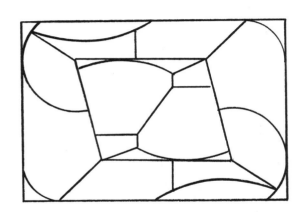

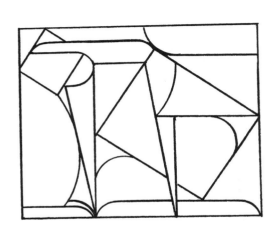

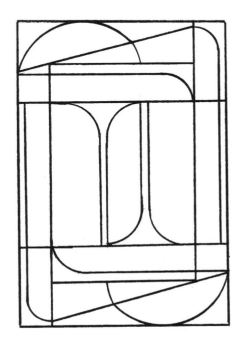

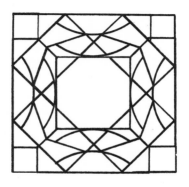

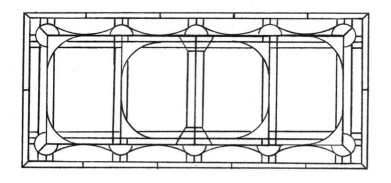

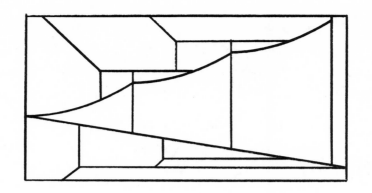

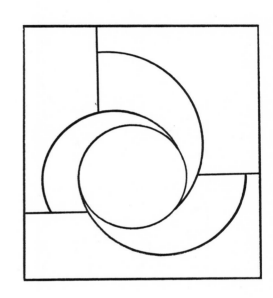

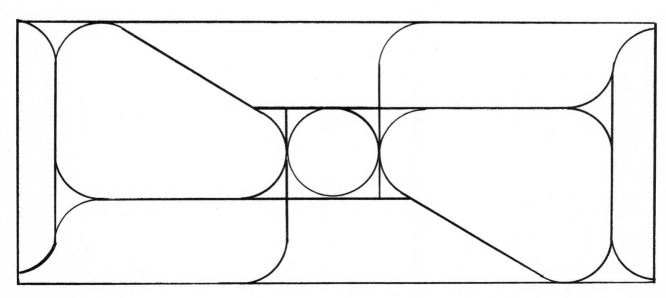

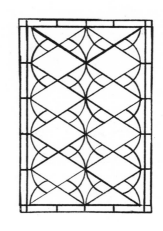
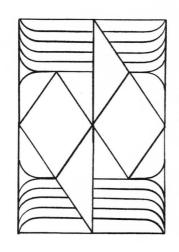

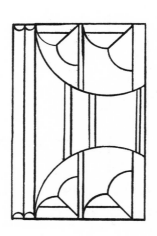

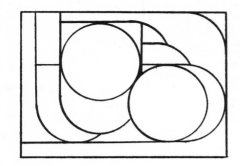

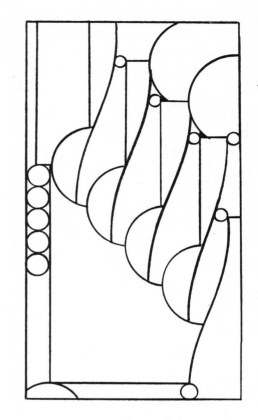

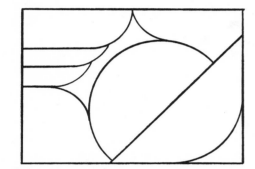

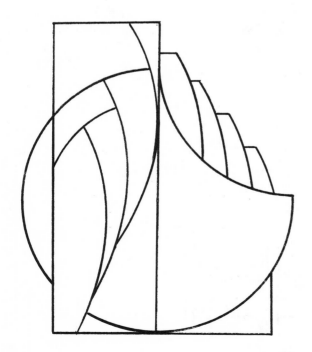

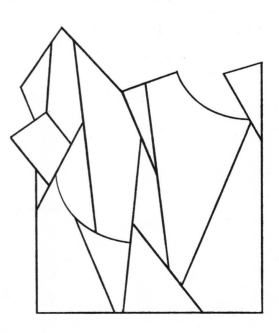

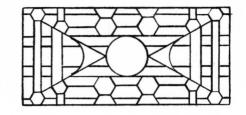

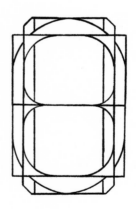

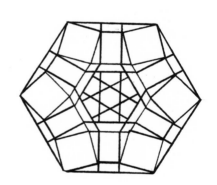

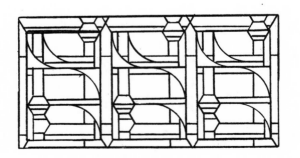

18

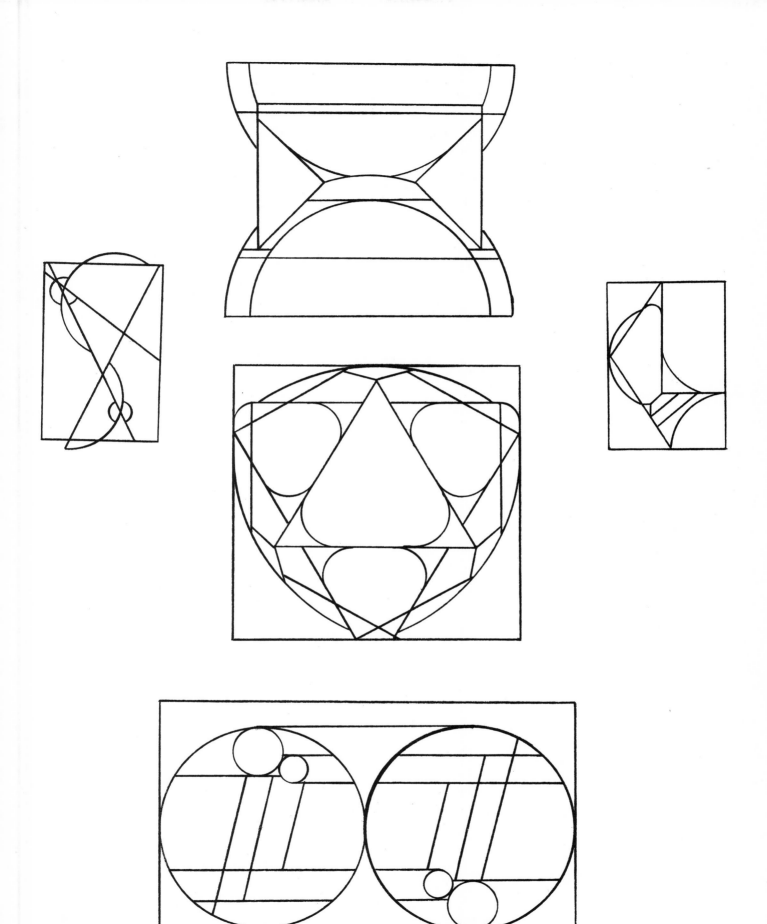

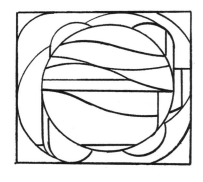

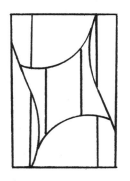

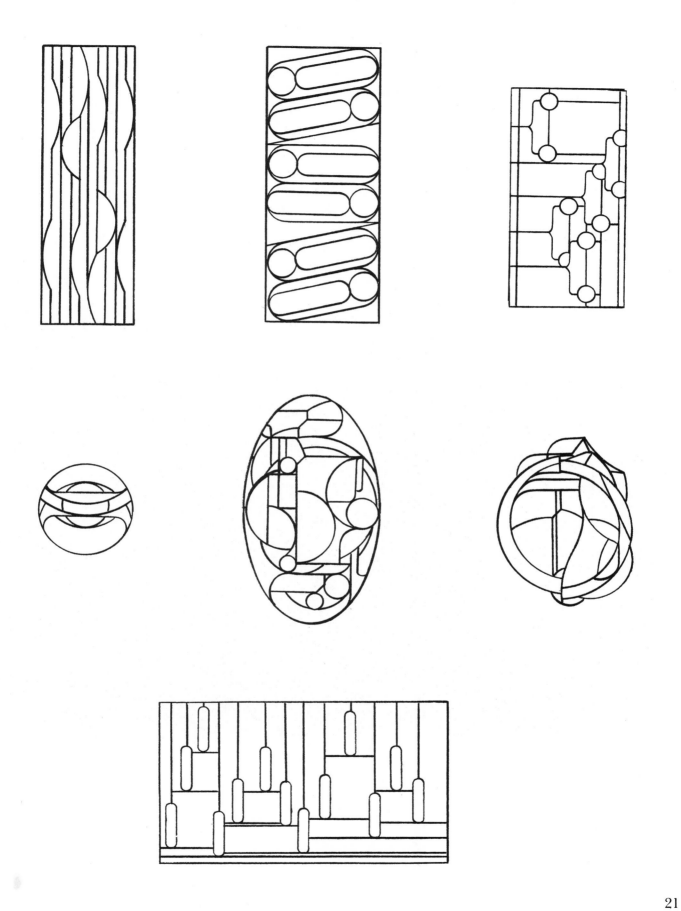

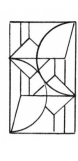

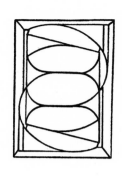
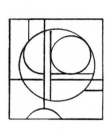
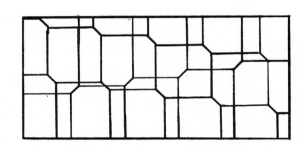

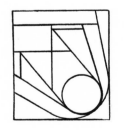
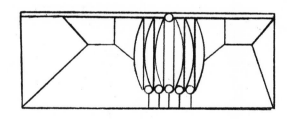

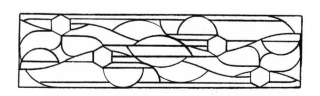
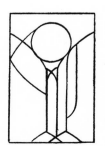

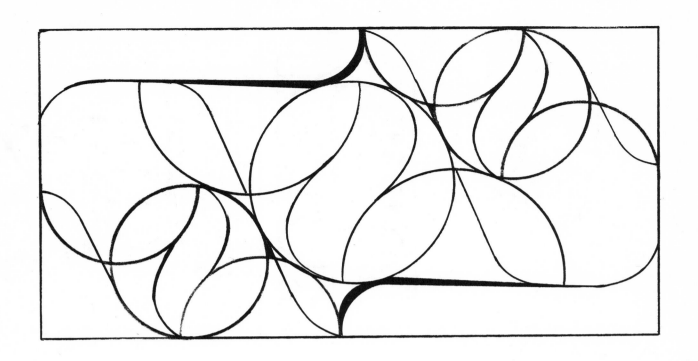

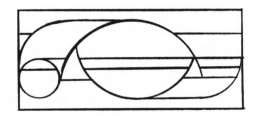

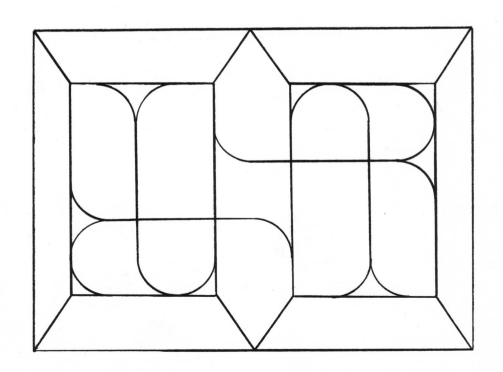

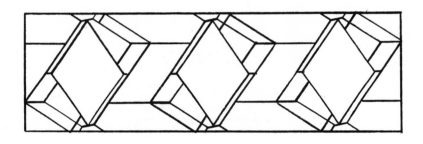

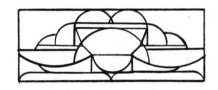

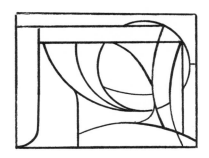

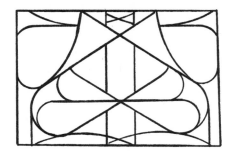

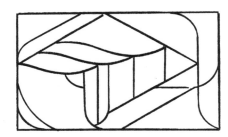

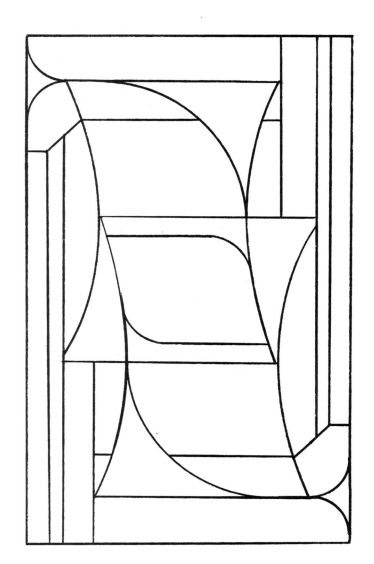

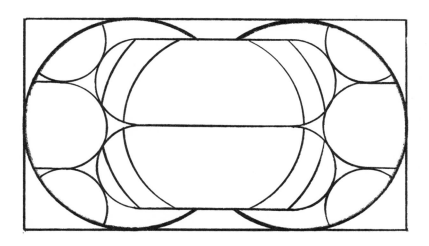

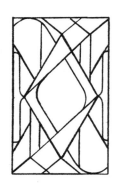

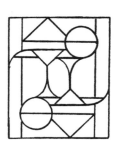

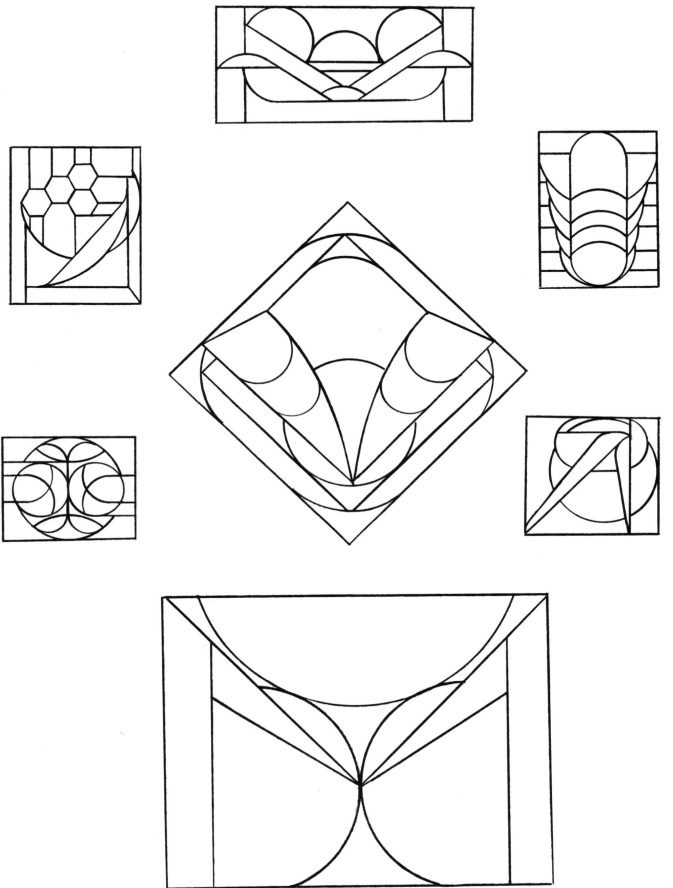

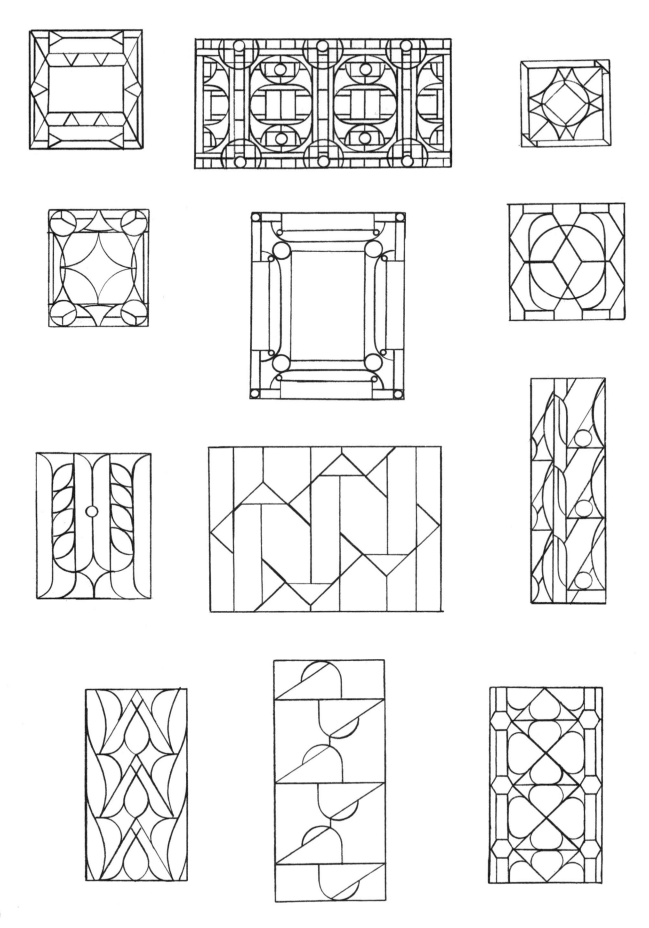

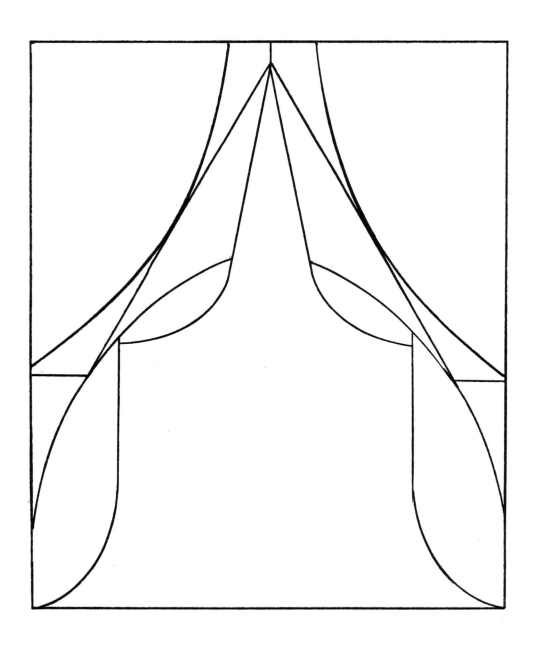

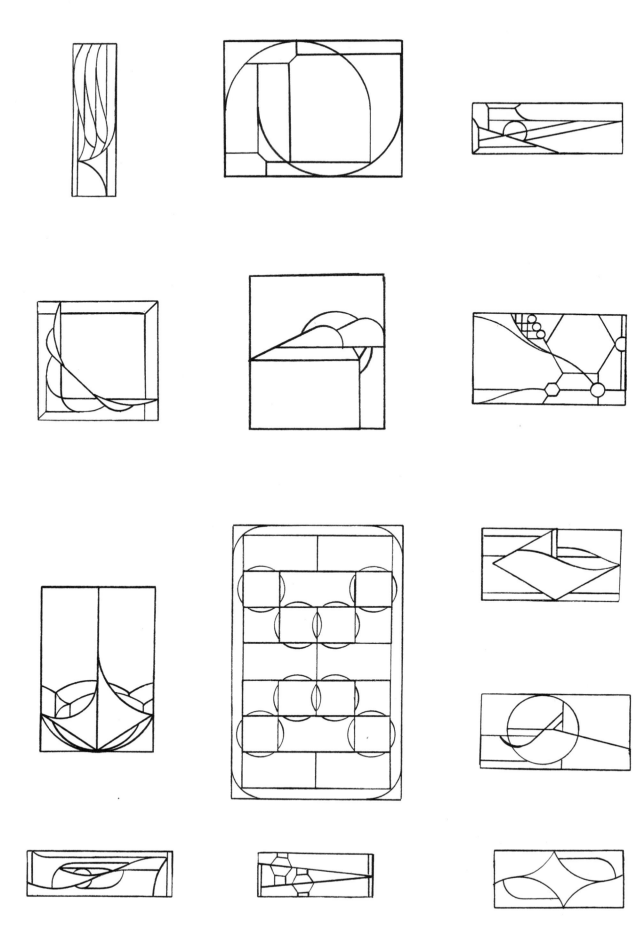

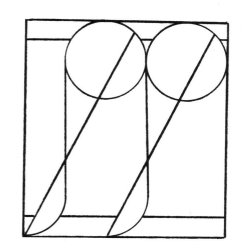

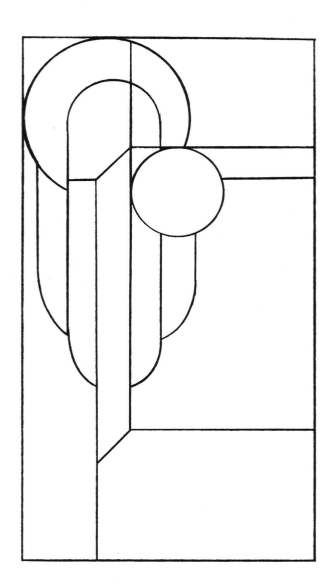

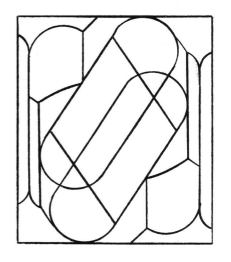

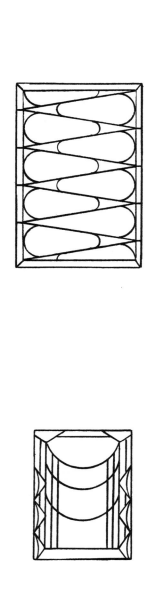
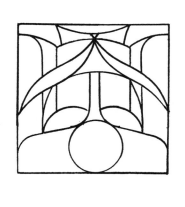

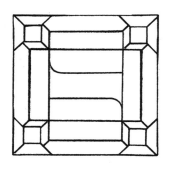

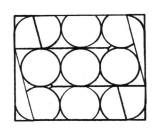
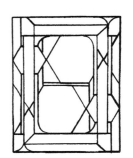
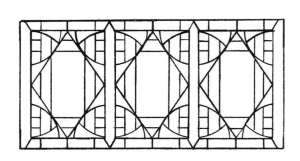

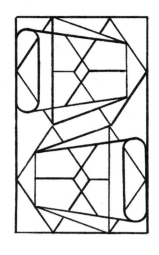
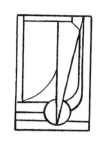

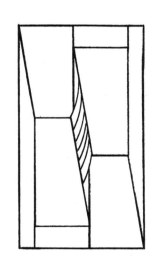

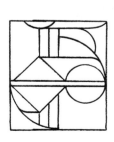
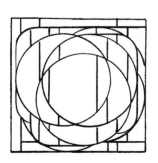

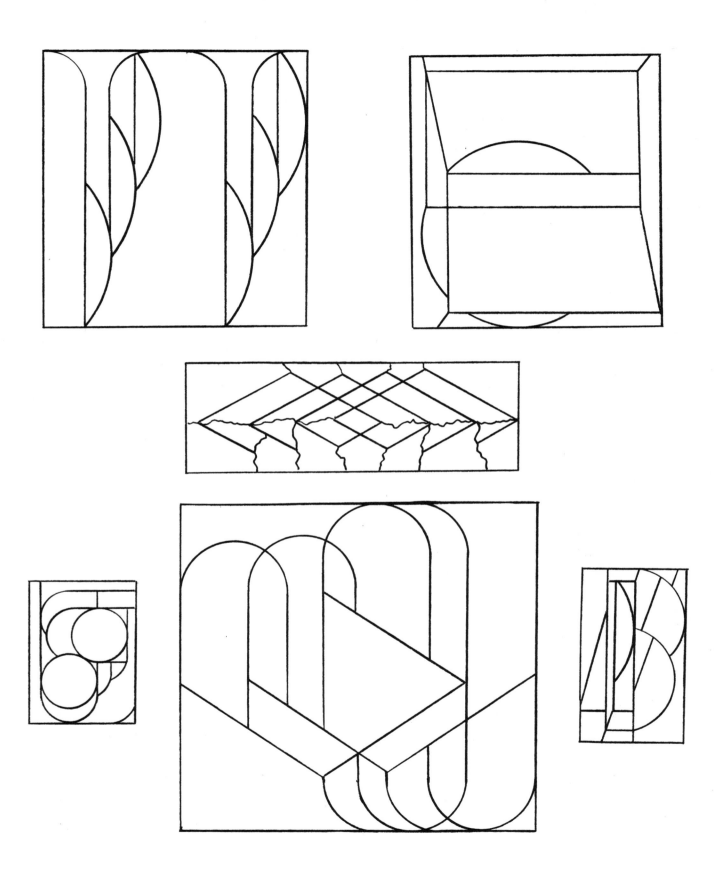

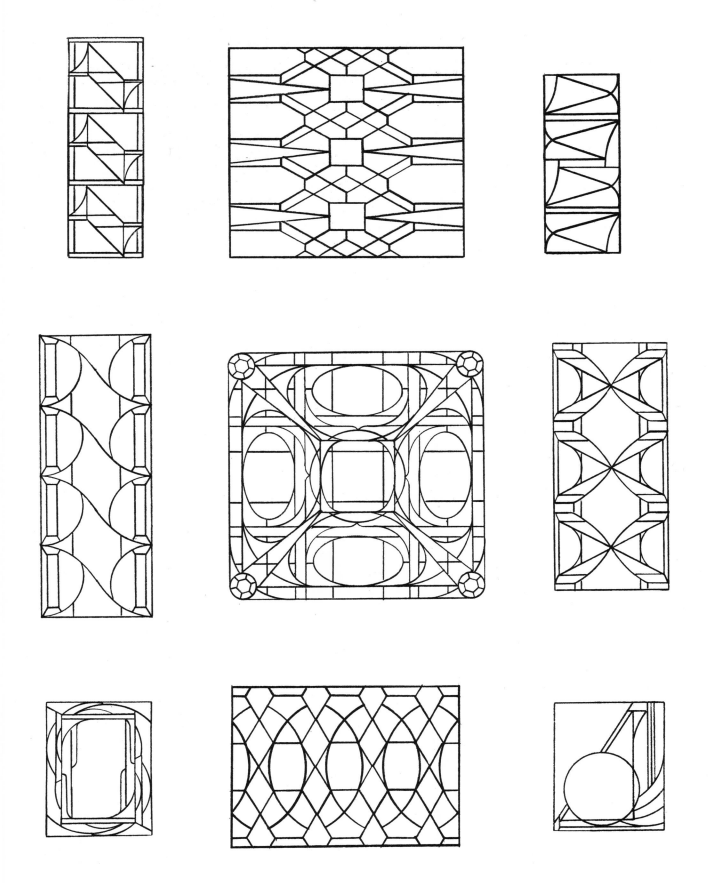

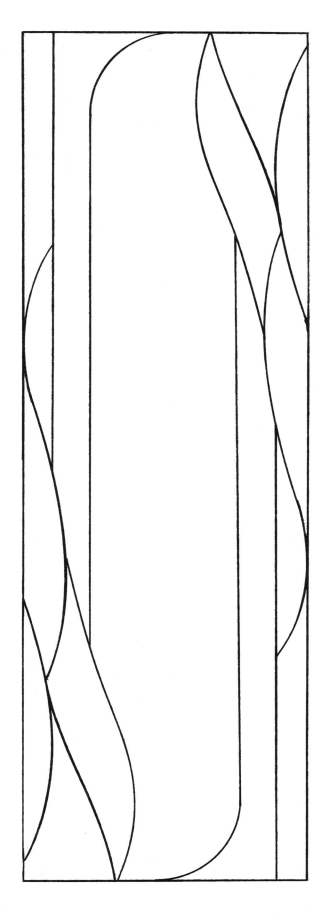

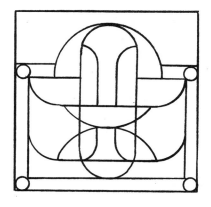

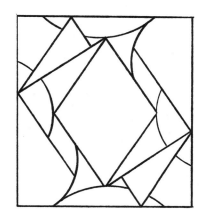

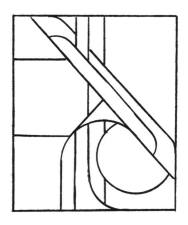

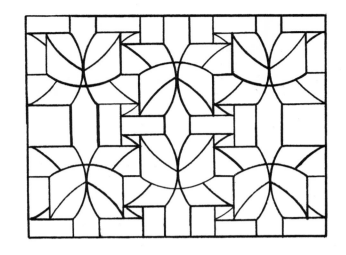

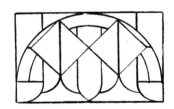

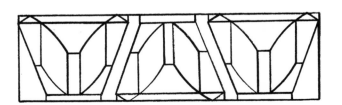

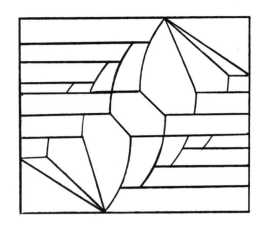

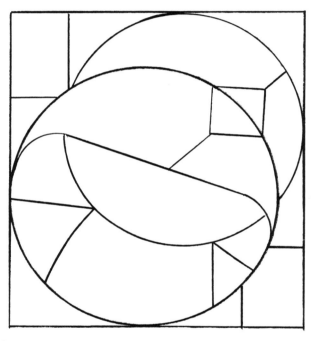

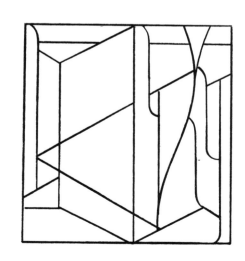

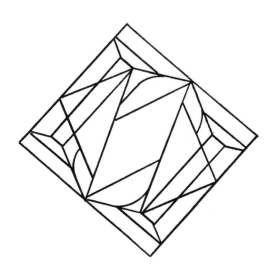

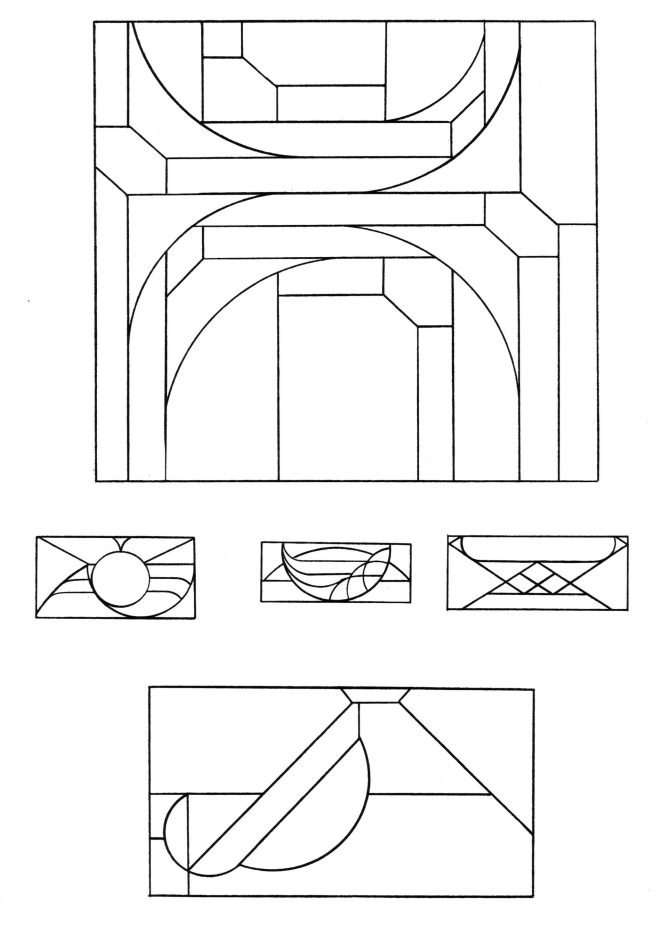

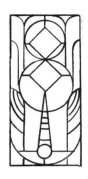

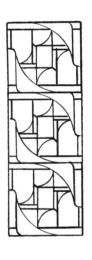

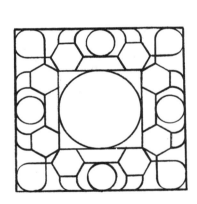

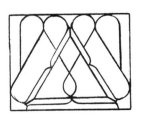

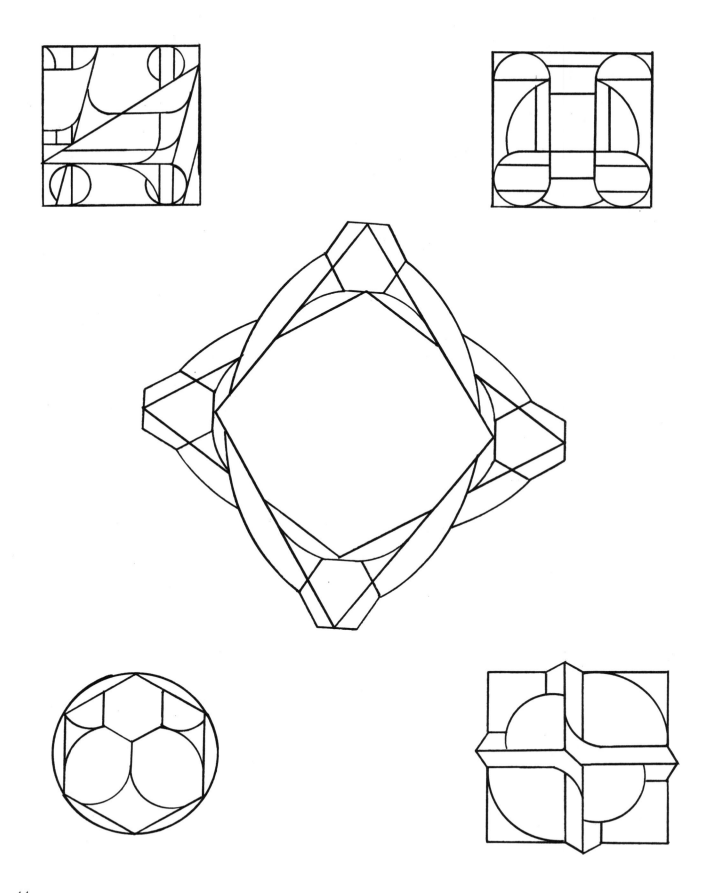

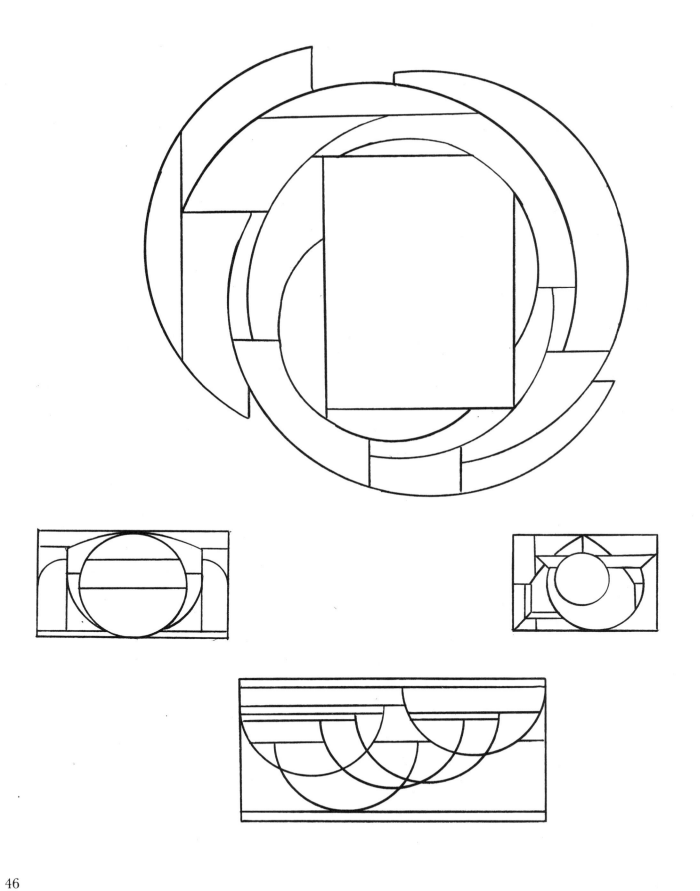

46

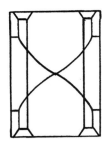

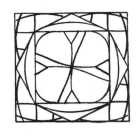

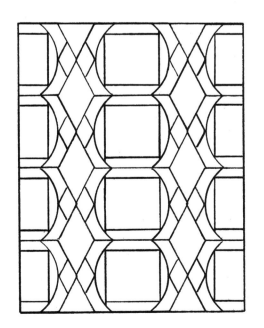

48

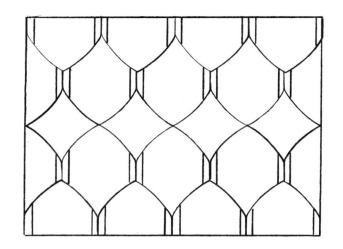

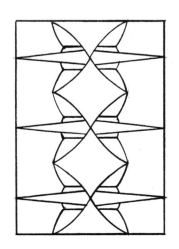

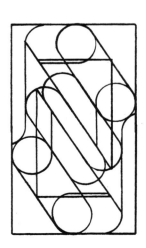

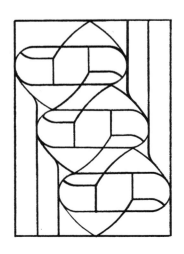

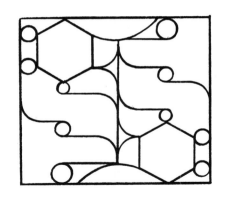

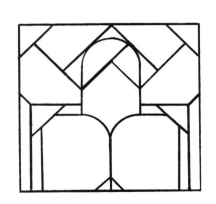

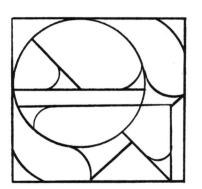

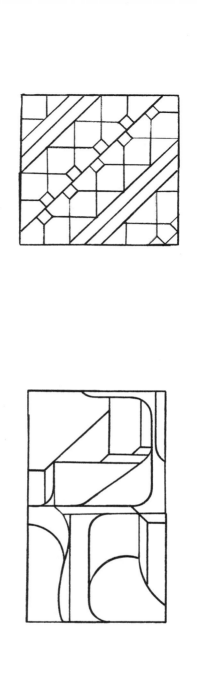
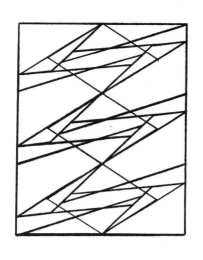
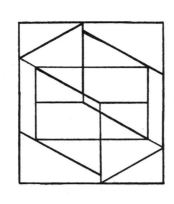
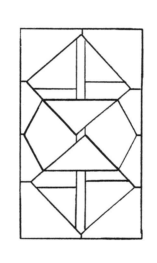
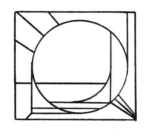

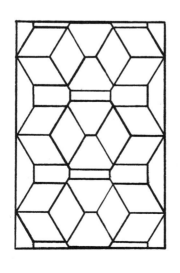
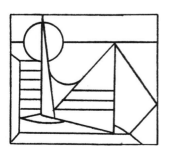

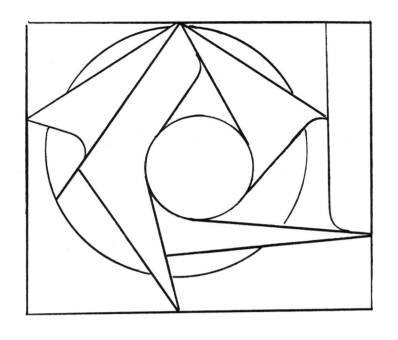

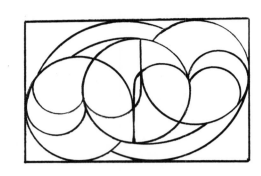

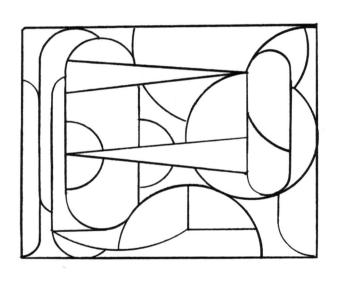

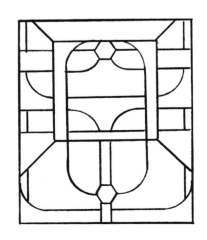

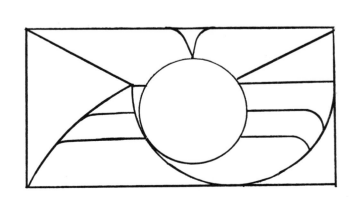

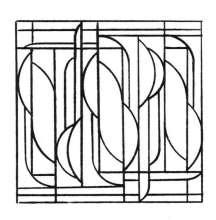

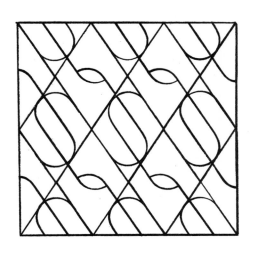
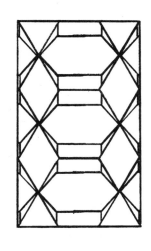
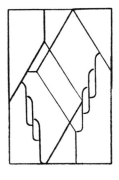
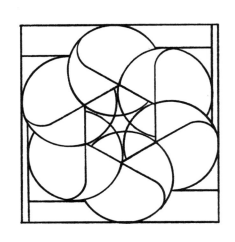

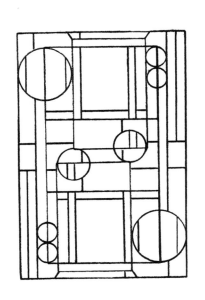
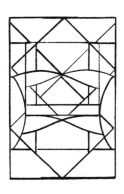

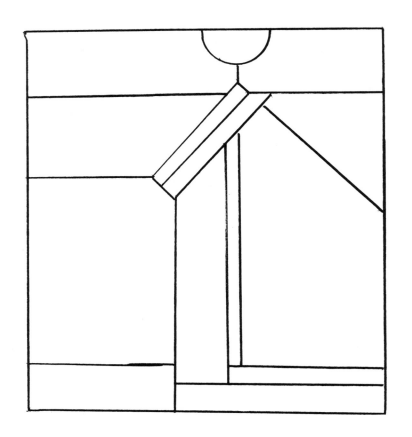

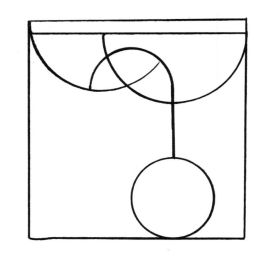

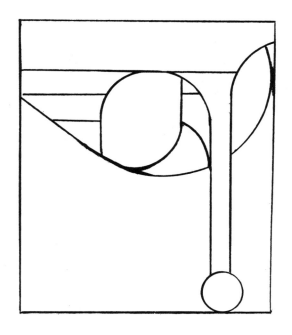

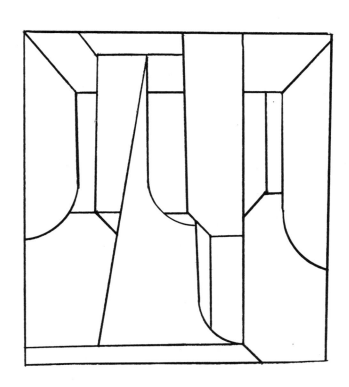

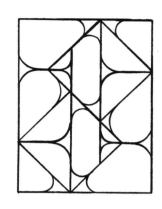

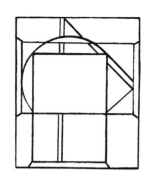

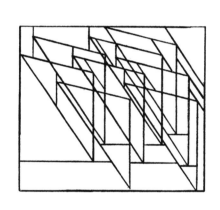

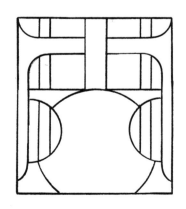

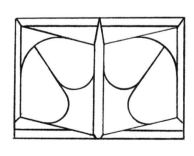

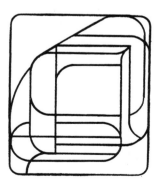

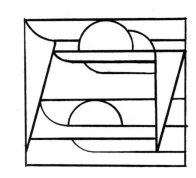

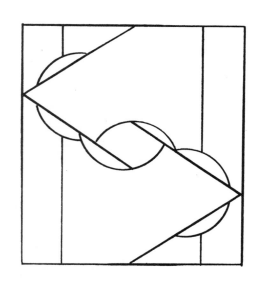

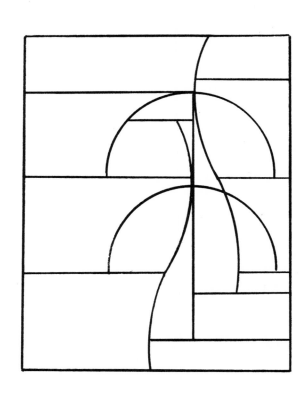

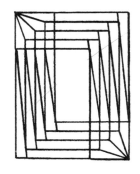
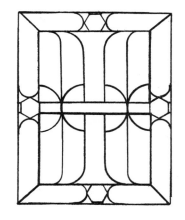

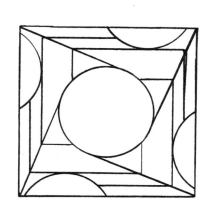
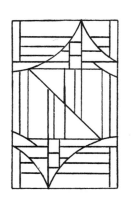

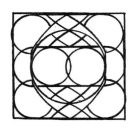

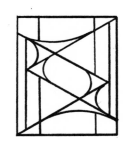

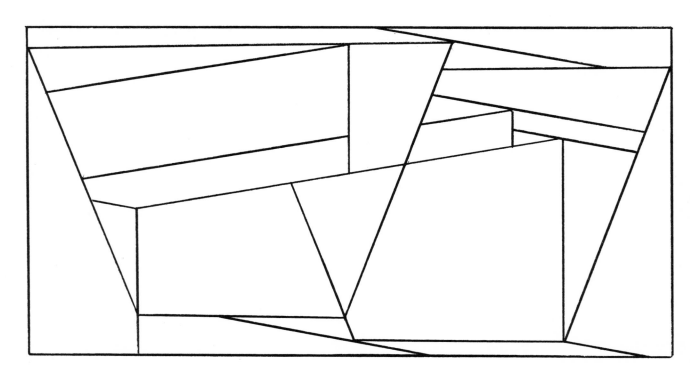